AF291389

The Scent of Your Shadow

SINU VARJU LÕHN

Kristiina Ehin
The Scent of Your Shadow

SINU VARJU LÕHN

Translated by Ilmar Lehtpere
Introduced by Sujata Bhatt

Arc
PUBLICATIONS
2010

Published by Arc Publications,
Nanholme Mill, Shaw Wood Road
Todmorden OL14 6DA, UK
www.arcpublications.co.uk

Design by Tony Ward
Printed in Great Britain by Lightning Source

978 1906570 53 8 (pbk)
978 1906570 54 5 (hbk)

Acknowledgements
The poems in this book have been selected from
Emapuhkus (Tallinn: Pandekt, 2009).
The author and translator gratefully acknowledge grants from
the Cultural Endowment of Estonia.
Some of these translations first appeared in
Modern Poetry in Translation and *Cyphers*.

Front cover illustration: © Kristiina Ehin 2010
Back cover illustration: © Eliisa Ehin 2010

**Arc Publications 'Visible Poets' series
Editor: Jean Boase-Beier**

CONTENTS

Series Editor's Note / 7
Translator's Preface / 9
Introduction / 12

I
Soe elu jäämäe jalamil /
Warm Life at the Foot of the Iceberg

20 / "Meie kodu on üleni…" • "Our home is entirely…" / 21
24 / "Mu ema ütleb…" • "My mother says…" / 25
30 / Hanereas • One by One / 31
32 / "Muutun hämaruse tulekuga…" • "With the coming of dusk…" / 33
36 / "Õed armsad õed…" • "Sisters dear sisters…" / 37
40 / "Merest tulevad lehmad…" • "Cows come from the sea…" / 41
44 / "Kaldapääsukesed merekivimustad…" • "Sand martins sea-stone black…" / 45
46 / "Laps mängib…" • "The child plays…" / 47

II
Su silmad mu sees / Your Eyes inside Me

52 / "Ootan sind seiklejat rännuhullu…" • "I wait for you adventurer mad rover…" / 53
54 / "Sellel ööl…" • "In that night…" / 55
56 / "Enam ei anna ma sulle rinda…" • "I don't give you my breast anymore…" / 57
58 / "Laps turnib aknalaual…" • "My child clambers on the windowsill…" / 59

60 / "Tunda on valgete hobuste lõhna…" • "The smell of white horses can be felt…" / 61

64 / "Mu puhkus oli lühike…" • "My holiday was short…" / 65

68 / "Lumi mäletab mu turja…" • "The snow remembers my shoulders…" / 69

III
Ronka ja päikest / Raven and Sun

72 / "Kihutan sinu poole…" • "I career along towards you…" / 73

78 / "Võtan pruudikleidi seljast…" • "I take off my bridal dress…" / 79

82 / "Su saarepuud…" • "Your ash trees…" / 83

84 / "Las trammid kaovad…" • "Let the trams disappear…" / 85

88 / "Terve kuhi kulda…" • "A whole pile of gold…" / 89

92 / Äralend • Flying Away / 93

94 / "Meil kõigil tuleb harjuda…" • "We all have to grow accustomed…" 95

96 / "Aed on täis…" • "The garden is full…" / 97

98 / "Vaatad mulle otsa…" • "You look at me…" / 99

Biographical Notes / 104

The 'Visible Poets' series was established in 2000, and set out to challenge the view that translated poetry could or should be read without regard to the process of translation it had undergone. Since then, things have moved on. Today there is more translated poetry available and more debate on its nature, its status, and its relation to its original. We know that translated poetry is neither English poetry that has mysteriously arisen from a hidden foreign source, nor is it foreign poetry that has silently rewritten itself in English. We are more aware that translation lies at the heart of all our cultural exchange; without it, we must remain artistically and intellectually insular.

One of the aims of the series was, and still is, to enrich our poetry with the very best work that has appeared elsewhere in the world. And the poetry-reading public is now more aware than it was at the start of this century that translation cannot simply be done by anyone with two languages. The translation of poetry is a creative act, and translated poetry stands or falls on the strength of the poet-translator's art. For this reason 'Visible Poets' publishes only the work of the best translators, and gives each of them space, in a Preface, to talk about the trials and pleasures of their work.

From the start, 'Visible Poets' books have been bilingual. Many readers will not speak the languages of the original poetry but they, too, are invited to compare the look and shape of the English poems with the originals. Those who can are encouraged to read both. Translation and original are presented side-by-side because translations do not displace the originals; they shed new light on them and are in turn themselves illuminated by the presence of their source poems. By drawing the readers' attention to the act of translation itself, it is the aim of these books to make the work of both the original poets and their translators more visible.

Jean Boase-Beier

In translating Kristiina Ehin's poetry I have the great good fortune of translating the work of the poet I admire most in any language. Not many translators are able to say this. The roots of Kristiina's very contemporary poetry are embedded deep in an ancient folk song tradition and in her organic view of the world. Like folk song, she invites the reader to share her experience at a primal level. The apparent but deceptive simplicity and directness of her language and her use of timeless imagery that bypasses the intellect and goes straight to the soul have enormous power, especially in our rootless, superficial times. Her subject matter is universal, yet deeply personal, and is expressed so vividly that her joys and sorrows seem to become one's own. Through Kristiina's poetry and prose I have begun to understand what it means to be a woman, to be a mother. Her work has lodged in my soul and I feel a great need to share it, to make it accessible to the English-speaking world.

I have been translating Kristiina's work – her poetry, prose and drama – since 2005 and have translated most of her published work and a fair bit of her as yet unpublished work as well. We have become close friends and this, along with my deep familiarity with her work, has attuned my ear very finely to her voice. One of the literary translator's most important tasks is to make the author's voice heard in translation. When I translate her work, I hear Kristiina's voice in my head and listen to her reading what I have written. If it sounds natural, if it sounds like her, I know it is right.

As a child of Estonian refugees I enjoyed a bilingual Estonian and English upbringing. Though I grew up far from Estonia, I lived in an Estonian community and had Estonia around me all the time in its language, mentality, humour, food, celebrations, songs, stories and the trauma of its history. Estonian was spoken at home, but at the age of five, in the summer before I started school, I learnt English – without trying, without even noticing, as young children are able to do. I wasn't even consciously aware of the vast conceptual differences between the two languages – the fourteen cases in Estonian, the lack of articles, the existence of only one third person pronoun, the lack of the verb 'to have' to name but a few – until I made my first tentative translations of poetry and folk tales when I was at university. I had learnt these languages independently of each other and until then had had no need to compare their structures.

But I was very much aware of the cultural differences from a very young age. All this formed my Estonian identity, an identity often at odds with my surroundings until I came home to Estonia for good three years ago. It was a true homecoming. This identity that I share with Kristiina gives me a deeper, instinctive understanding of her work and the culture her work is embedded in, an understanding I strive to convey in my translations of her work. At the same time, translating Kristiina's poetry and prose has also been, and continues to be, a journey of discovery and an exploration of my own identity, which stems largely from the Supilinn (Souptown) district of Tartu, where the house that used to belong to my grandfather, the house my father lived in so long ago is literally a stone's throw away from Kristiina's flat.

Kristiina's very contemporary poetry is imbued with folklore and folk song and hence with fundamental human experience. She increasingly makes use of folk music in her readings and incorporates traditional *regilaul*, a two thousand year-old, still living form of Estonian folk song, in some of her poems.

Continuity is central to her work, indeed she has said that she regards herself as heir to the ancient Estonian tradition of female singer-poets. Elsewhere I have written that her poetry spans centuries, millennia. That it is at once modern and primeval. There is a timeless quality to her work, and this of course applies to her use of language as well. Her work is inclusive, appealing to a broad cross-section of people in Estonia and beyond – the increasing popularity of her poetry and prose beyond Estonia's borders is also evidence of this. In her frequent appearances abroad she reads and sings her poetry in English, thereby making direct contact with her audience. Rooted as her work is in Estonian culture, its appeal is nevertheless universal, touching her readers and listeners deeply and personally through these roots that contribute to the cultural diversity that enriches us and the world we live in.

As Kristiina's English language translator, I feel an enormous sense of responsibility in conveying her work in its many facets to the English-speaking world, and therefore essentially to the rest of the world as well.

Ilmar Lehtpere

These translations are dedicated to my wife Sadie Murphy.

INTRODUCTION:
A GENEROUS, HONEST IMAGINATION

The first time I met Kristiina Ehin was in November 2001, in Stockholm, where we were participants at an international poetry festival. One of my first impressions of her was her warmth and openness, her strong stage presence and her poise. Seven years later, I met Kristiina again, this time in Raplamaa, Estonia, as her guest at the first 'Full Moon Poetry Festival' which she had organised with her parents, the distinguished, highly esteemed poets, Ly Seppel and Andres Ehin. This festival brought together poets, songwriters, singers and musicians from near and far and from very diverse places such as Japan, Ireland, Shetland and Hungary. One of the striking features of this festival was the rural setting: Luhtre Farm and Haimre Village Hall, deep in the heart of the countryside, places dense with trees through which we would look for the moon, the full moon.

Kristiina opened the evenings by singing *regilaul* which she had composed; on other occasions, she also shared her poetry with us. Once again, I was struck by the musicality of her performance, and by her warmth and generous hospitality as she introduced us, the foreign visitors, to the culture, traditions, and history of Estonia.

Listening to her reading, I was happily reminded of the power of an oral tradition, which is just as important as a written tradition, and of the fact that poetry is an oral art as much as it is a written art. Kristiina Ehin is clearly grounded in a rich oral tradition. Indeed, my impression of Estonian poets is that they are closer to the folklore, storytelling and song traditions than poets elsewhere in Europe. Perhaps one of the reasons for this is that all those who were writing and even speaking the language of the people had to experience severe clashes and struggles with the oppressor's tongue. Now, after having achieved freedom, one can feel the drive of Estonian writers to reach out to the world, which had been blocked away from them, and to participate in the discourse of international poetry. A poet such as Kristiina Ehin truly has something to add to the chorus of voices. Indeed, she has said: "I've long dreamt of organising the poetry festival that I would like to be invited to. A poetry festival that would bring people together in some beautiful place in the countryside, a festival that would naturally unite poetry and song as one and would make Estonians conscious of the fact that by virtue of the existence of Estonian *regilaul*, we are not only an ancient nation of song, but an ancient nation of poetry as well."

Although this was my first visit to Estonia, I felt strangely at home amongst people who believe in sacred trees, sacred stones and sacred places, people who in this respect reminded me of certain members of my own family. It was an uncanny experience for me to feel both at home and to feel the 'exotic, foreign otherness' of Estonian culture.

The 'Full Moon Poetry Festival' was one of the most intense and extraordinary festivals that I have ever taken part in. Indeed, I find it difficult to say what I enjoyed most: the conversations with the other poets, listening to the musicians rehearse, the evening performances followed by bonfires, the visit to the Sillaotsa Farm Museum where we learnt about the traditional process of baking bread and where Kristiina taught us some of the basic steps of Estonian folk dances, or the journey deep into the forest that led out to the sea. During the walk in the forest, I particularly enjoyed the quiet, private moments I was able to share with Ly Seppel, Kristiina and Kristiina's young son, who is one of the Muses for both *Emapuhkus* and *The Scent of Your Shadow*. *Emapuhkus* is the original Estonian book from which this collection is drawn.

Among other things, the Festival Charter states: "Creating poetry was not just some private, personal matter for Estonians, but a communal activity and shared joy of creation full of collective power." And we, the foreign guests, were tremendously lucky to be able to participate in such communal activities and to truly share our work with each other in informal ways as well as the formal performances. I should add that Luhtre Farm was an amazing place to be: the excellent, home-cooked food, (not to forget the very special home-brewed beer), the clear air, fragrant with fir trees, and the remarkable sauna, which is also an essential part of Estonian culture. Many of us simply found no time or desire to sleep, as we didn't want to miss a moment of anything.

There was nothing contrived or false about this Festival just as there is nothing contrived or false about Kristiina's work. One could feel her sensitive, caring, sisterly and motherly presence in all the details of the organisation; nothing was neglected, wasted, ignored or otherwise left to careless chance. Kristiina Ehin is a young woman of many talents: besides being a poet and a singer, she has written short stories and a play, and has also worked as a journalist, a translator, a dance teacher and a nature reserve warden. And judging by the exquisite covers of her books, she is a formidable visual artist as well. Her poetry is no doubt informed and enriched by all of these skills and experiences, these very different ways of interacting with life. Hers is a generous, honest imagination: visceral, shamanistic and wise. She is a visionary poet with a discerning and distinctive voice, a voice resonant with genuine passion, close to the primordial world of spirits and myths but also rooted in history and in contemporary life. Kristiina is unafraid of exploring the complex and difficult aspects of human relationships and at the same time she is funny, witty, and of course, musical. There is a refreshing lightness and originality to her poems, which are nonetheless poignant. She is able to express strong emotions without being sentimental. Her work has truly haunted me; it has entered the deepest layer of my being with its rare combination of directness and subtle nuances, ancient traditions and modernity. Somehow, she is able 'to say' what can't be said. The integrity, courage and authenticity of Kristiina's writing naturally stems from her own soul, her own life. It is not surprising that her work has been received with great acclaim, both in her native country and abroad.

In Kristiina Ehin's biographical note at the end of this book, we learn that 'the poems were written over a period of two years beginning shortly before the birth of her child'. This is a natural time frame in the lives of many women, and a time frame that many new mothers who work on creative projects in the arts choose to focus on. What is unique here is the manner in which Kristiina has portrayed her two years: the way her fierce mother's love breathes within her startling, energetic imagery. The landscape in these poems seems to be under a spell, a spell cast by the transformative power of a mother's gaze. There is also sorrow and anger, deeply felt sorrow and anger, and yet, these poems are a tonic, a tonic against the world-weary, facile, ironic gestures displayed by so many writers today. Reading Kristiina's poems, somehow I feel as if I am reading the work of a younger sister, or a daughter, someone I have known all my life; I feel she is a kindred spirit despite the vast cultural differences that lie between us.

No poem can be adequately paraphrased or 'explained'. Here are some excerpts from her work, just some of the lines, out of many, that I have returned to again and again:

With the coming of dusk
and the dropping of leaves I become
more and more nocturnal

I become ever more thirsty
and from this thirst my thirst is fulfilled   (pp. 33 / 35)

   *

To become someone's own means being
dangerously close to a human star   (p. 41)

   *

I am empty
from the beauty of the purple streak in the sky
the horses of the mother of God
and the scent of your shadow
at the bottom of the valley   (p. 63)

   *

At the end of the wooden path
I burn with yearning for the real me   (p. 91)

   *

Yet where you were
where you were rooted
the sky was more sky-like   (p. 93)

   *

The garden is full
of the song of my white feet

My soul is like these threads of spider silk
tensed
criss-cross
between two apple trees   (p. 97)

   *

In me there is yellow and black
and raven and sun   (p. 99)

The best response to a poem is another poem, or a translation, and in this respect Ilmar Lehtpere has responded beautifully to Kristiina Ehin's work. As readers, we should be immensely grateful to him for having devoted such care and such profound empathy in his translations. Very few writers have the good fortune to engage with such a dedicated, meticulous translator, and very few translators have the chance to forge a close friendship with the writer they admire most. Here, I should add that Ilmar Lehtpere is also a fine poet in his own right and, (as mentioned above), Kristiina is also a translator; and so I believe that this contributes to their instinctive understanding of each other.

If one considers that translation, by necessity, is always a re-creation, where the new text requires a new life in the language it is translated into, then one can understand how a translation can never be a mere duplicate version of the original. Thus, *The Scent of Your Shadow* is a new book, drawing on a selection of poems from *Emapuhkus*, but different in its scope and trajectory. *Emapuhkus* has also been praised for its stunning design: besides Kristiina's poems, it incorporates prose passages, hand-written memoirs from Kristiina's female ancestors, as well as photographs of them. It is a beautiful book that would be valued by any bibliophile. Naturally, for some of us, this might awaken the desire to learn Estonian. Until then, however, we can rely on Ilmar Lehtpere.

Readers in the UK and Ireland may well be familiar with Kristiina Ehin's poems and short stories, since this is not her first book to appear in English translation.

And needless to say, already, I am looking forward to Kristiina's next book, be it poetry or prose.

Sujata Bhatt

I
WARM LIFE AT THE FOOT OF THE ICEBERG

SOE ELU JÄÄMÄE JALAMIL

¶

Meie kodu on üleni
sirelipõõsaisse uppunud
nii et eemalt paistab vaid katuseviil
Need Eestimaa vanad
viilkatusega alevimajad
on kõik nii sarnased
sadade tuhandete viisi
et ei saagi aru
miks pidada üht kallimaks kui teist
Köögiaken ikka tänava poole
vaskne lipuvardatoru
sini-valge majanumber
aiavärav postkast uksekell
suviti õhuakendel sääsevõrgud ees
kojas kummikud
ja aiatöökindad
Pilved kihutamas üle õuemuru
mille väärtust ei saa
millegagi mõõta

Ainult see mürin
see lõputu autode mürin
trügib üha lähemale
saab järjest varahommikusemaks
järjest hilisõhtusemaks
ja südapäeval käin juba ammu ringi
kõrvaklapid peas

Vanaisa ehitas maja munakivitee äärde
aga nüüd möirgab siin
maantee

¶

Our home is entirely
submerged in lilac bushes
so that from a distance only the gable shows
These old Estonian
gable-roofed market-town houses
are all so similar
in their hundreds of thousands
that you can't understand
why one should be held more dear than another
Kitchen window always facing the street
copper flagstaff holder
blue-white house number
garden-gate letterbox doorbell
in summer mosquito netting in front of the airing windows
wellies in the hall
and gardening gloves
clouds racing over the lawn
whose worth can't
be measured in any way

Only this rumbling
this endless rumbling of cars
presses ever closer
becomes constantly more early-morning
constantly more late-evening
and by day I've long been going round
wearing headphones

Grandfather built this house beside a cobblestone road
But now what roars past
is a main road

Nägin unes et selle maantee asemel
voolab meie maja ees
lai jõgi
päris ehtne jõgi
pärlendav päikesekollane rahulik
kaldad pärlikarpe täis nagu
enne Katariina II aega

Korjasin emale peotäie
ilusaid valusaid jõepärleid
Lasksime isaga õnged
köögiaknast otse jõkke
saime ahvenaid ja kammeljaid
Köök sai magusat praelõhna täis

Ema kael ja käeseljad helendasid
pärlite paistuses
Sõime jõge vaadates kala
ja rüüpasime kalja peale
siin oma
viilkatuse ja sirelipõõsaste all

See unenäojõgi oma kalade ja pärlitega
ei lähe mul meelest

I had a dream that in place of the main road
a river flows past our house
a wide river
a quite genuine river
sparkling yellow from the sun serene
its banks full of pearl mussels like
before Catherine II's time

For Mother I gathered a handful
of beautiful dazzling river pearls
Father and I cast our fishing rods
from the kitchen window straight into the river
we caught perch and turbot
The kitchen filled with the sweet smell of frying

Mother's neck and hands brightened
in the pearls' glow
We ate fish while looking at the river
and sipped kvass
here beneath
our own gable roof and lilac bushes

That dream with its fish and pearls
will not leave my mind

¶

Mu ema ütleb et
peaksin sinuga abielluma
Aga sina pole isegi palunud mu kätt

Joome emaga lennukis veini
kuskil Poola või Slovakkia kohal
ja ta räägib mulle
kuidas ta korraldaks meie pulmad
vanaaegsed pulmad pruudikodust lahkumisega
Juba ta mõtleb keda kutsuda
juba ta mõtleb mida pakkuda
juba ta mõtleb kus kirikus oleks laulatus

Ja minagi vajun mõttesse

Mu sõbrannad tuleksid ju kokku ja laulaksid
säält sa löüdse uma õnnõ kuldnõ noorik
üüse hüä om hõlma võtta kuldnõ noorik
päivä hüä om pääle kaia kuldnõ noorik

Ja mu õde tuleks ja laulaks
Õekene minu õeke
Nüüd hakkad sina ju minema
Nüüd hakkavad uksed uluma
seinapraod praksuma
Kus sa nutad nurgad märjad
kus sa astud asemed märjad
kus sa seisad seinad märjad

Ja minu sugulased laulaksid
Meie pruuti piimal pestud

¶

My mother says
I should marry you
But you haven't even asked for my hand

My mother and I drink wine in a plane
somewhere over Poland or Slovakia
and she tells me
how she would organise our wedding
an old-time wedding with taking leave of the bride's home
She's already thinking about who to invite
she's already thinking about what to offer
she's already thinking about which church to have the ceremony in

And even I sink into thought

My girl friends would come together and sing
there you've lit upon your own joy golden young bride
good to hold close in the nighttime golden young bride
good to look at in the daytime golden young bride

And my sister would come and sing
Sister dear my sister dear
Now you're ready to start going
Now the doors will all start wailing
cracks in the walls cracking open
Where you weep the corners get wet
where you step the beds do get wet
where you stand the walls do get wet

And my relatives would sing
Our bride has been bathed in milk

piimal pestud võil valatud
noorel koorel klopitud
tallelihaga toidetud
Küll on valge merevahtu
valgem veel on meie pruuti
Küll on sirge sillalauda
sirgem veel on meie pruuti

Ja sinu sugulased laulaksid
Kas on rikas Riia linna
rikkam veel on meie peigu
Tamm on tammikus tugeva
tugevam veel meie peigu

Ja siis laulaksid kõik koos
pikkade vanaaegsete venitustega
Tehke lahti laiad uksed
valged vestetud väravad
Ja me sõidaksime välja
tagasi vaatamata

Aga emale ütlen veini rüübates
Jätame nüüd selle jutu
ta pole veel isegi...

Ja me hakkame rääkima hoopis Alpidest
mis juba terenduvad kaugel all
ja kahekümnekraadisest mereveest
mis meid Vahemeres ees ootab

bathed in milk the butter poured
freshest cream been whisked up for her
given meat of kid goat to eat
White indeed may be the sea foam
whiter by far is our bride
Straight indeed may be the bridge planks
straighter by far is our bride

And your relatives would sing
Riga town is ever so rich
richer by far our bridegroom
Oak is strong amid the oakwood
stronger by far our bridegroom

And then they would all sing together
stretching out the words as of old
Open up wide the wide doors now
open the white whittled gates now
And we would ride out
without looking back

But sipping wine I say to my mother
Let's leave it now
he hasn't even…

And we start to talk about the Alps instead
which are already looming far below
and the twenty-degree sea water
waiting for us in the Mediterranean

Varsti jääb ema poolelt sõnalt magama
sirge seljaga nagu kaelkirjak
mu pisike poeg süles
Imetlen tema võimet
magada ükskõik kus ja millal
Võib-olla peakski selle võime omandamiseks
abielluma
Või ei tohiks selle kartuses just kunagi
abielluda

Ostsin hiljuti valgete lintidega linased
hermesekingad
Need sobiksid minusugusele pruudile
Veel polegi ma väga vana
näen välja mitte palju üle kahekümne viie
Kui sa pole abielus olnud
ei saa sa õieti kunagi teada
mis tunne see on
oli ema öelnud

Igatahes ei tuleks meil mingit nukumähkimist
ega puupaku lõhkumist
Ainult kurepesapuu külge seoksime lindi
mu uljaste hermesekingade küljest

Juba oleksimegi sinu väravas
Sul oleks mu poeg kukil
Astuksime koos sinu aeda
kus klaariõunad ja naerid
on just küpseks saanud

Soon my mother falls asleep in mid-word
straight-backed as a giraffe
my little son in her lap
I wonder at her ability
to sleep anywhere and anytime
Maybe to acquire this ability I should
marry
Or for fear of it never
marry

Recently I bought a pair of linen hermes shoes
with white ribbons
They would suit a bride like me
I'm still not very old yet
I don't look much over twenty-five
*If you've never been married
you can't ever really know
what it feels like*
my mother had said

In any case for us there would be no putting nappies on a doll for the bride
and splitting wood for the groom
We would only tie a ribbon from my daring hermes shoes
to a tree with a stork's nest in it

We would already be at your gate
You'd have my son on your shoulders
We'd step into your garden together
where the yellow apples and turnips
have only just ripened

HANEREAS

Neiud kui me lähme haprad küünlakroonid peas
jalga jala ette tõstes taha vaatamata
riime eirates ja ettearvamatust kiites
tee peal naiseks saades või ka mitte iial
Neiud kui me lähme haprad küünlakroonid peas
paju puistab punalehti meie jalge ette
öö on ümber piha ümber metsa põllu luha
külm ei ole pugenud veel sügavale põue
Neiud kui me lähme haprad küünlakroonid peas
tuleb ette hundiraudu bensujaamu pätte
Mõni maha jääb kuid teised vaatavad vaid ette
enda ette igavesti hanereas

ONE BY ONE

Maidens when we go with fragile candle crowns on our heads
putting one foot before the other not looking back
ignoring rhymes and exalting the unpredictable
becoming women on the way or else never at all
Maidens when we go with fragile candle crowns on our heads
the willow scatters red leaves before our feet
the night is around our shoulders around the forest marsh
the cold has not yet crept very deep into our breast
Maidens when we go with fragile candle crowns on our heads
we are met with the wolf trap of petrol station louts
Some are left behind but the others only look ahead
ahead forever one by one

¶

Muutun hämaruse tulekuga
ja lehtede langemisega
üha öisemaks
Olen üleni täis
selle suveõhtu nimetut üminat

Muutun üha öisemaks
ja ma ei vaja täna su lõket
su tunnetesüsist lõket
ennast soojendama

Muutun ühes hämarusega
valge sireli sarnaseks
meelespeasiniseks
lupiinlillaks
järjest suveöisemaks
selle vihmatu seitsmevennapäeva ööst öisemaks
vajun ikka sügavamale öö sülle
tagaaia nõgesepuhmaste vahele

Ma ei vaja täna su lõket
suure puhta kuu
võtan täna kaissu
ennast soendama
muutun järjest õhtusemaks
järjest paadisemaks
järjest neiumaks ja noormehemaks
sinisilmsemaks
ja piimjamaks
siin aias mis on täis
valge ristiku vahuharju
ja noorte öökullide huikeid

¶

With the coming of dusk
and the dropping of leaves I become
more and more nocturnal
I am brimming
with this summer evening's nameless hum

I become ever more nocturnal
and I don't need your fire today
the fire of the coals of your feelings
to warm myself

Together with the dusk I become
more like the white lilac
forget-me-not blue
lupin purple
ever more summer-night nocturnal
more nocturnal than this rainless Seven Brothers' Day night
I fall ever deeper into the lap of night
between the back garden's nettle bushes

I don't need your fire today
today I embrace
the big pure moon
to warm myself
I become more and more evening
ever more boat-like
more girlish and young-mannish
more blue-eyed
and milky
in this garden which is full
of foaming waves of white clover
and the hooting of young owls

Muutun järjest janusemaks
ja sellest janust saab mu janu täis
muutun järjest tõsisemaks
selle öö tõeks
järjest tumedamaks
sulnimaks
seitsmevennapäeva öö
õeks

I become ever more thirsty
and from this thirst my thirst is fulfilled
I become ever more serious
become the truth of this night
ever darker
more delightful
the sister
of this Seven Brothers' Day night

¶

Õed armsad õed
kõrvuti elu elajad
kõrvuti kontsade
kandjad
pikkade juuste sugejad
siidipäised ja sulnid
kõrvuti kurvastajad
armastajad
Õed armsad õed
õnnelikud ja tulised
unised nõiutud
õed

Kahe jalaga maas
sina mu vanem sõsar

sina mu noorem õeraas
pealael isetehtud vaas
surised ja õitsed

Õed armsad õed
tahaks teiega ühte laulda
pikas vooris läbi maalinna loogelda
Tahaks korraga näha
kui palju teid on
kuuvalgel tantsijaid
armastuseallikal
elujanu kustutajaid
kõrvuti tuhudest tõusjaid
kiirteel kihutajaid
paigalejääjaid ja põgenejaid
andjaid ja võtjaid

¶

Sisters dear sisters
side by side livers of life
side by side wearers
of heels
combers of long hair
silk-headed and sweet
side by side sorrowers
lovers
Sisters dear sisters
happy and fiery
sleepy bewitched
sisters

Both feet on the ground
you my older sister

You my younger bit of a sister
on your head a vase of your own making
you buzz and blossom

Sisters dear sisters
I want to sing as one with you
to meander in a long retinue through a hillfort
I'd like for once to see
how many of you there are
dancers by moonlight
quenchers of the thirst for life
at the spring of love
side by side risers from labour pains
speeders on fast roads
stayers and absconders
givers and takers

Me olem´ kolmeksi sõsare
Kus me kolmi kokku saame
kolmi kokku nelja ütte
kolmi kokku kukkumaie
nelja ütte laulamaie

We the three of us are sisters
Where will we three get together
three together four as one
three all cuckooing together
four of us all singing as one

¶

Merest tulevad lehmad
sel aegade alguse hommikul
sinirohelised lehmad
udarad soolast merepiima täis
Ja Mereema ajab nad kaldasse
mererohust vitsaga

Merineitsid tulge lehmi hoidma
ja ennast hoidma
iharate õitsiliste eest
Sada sinirohelist lehma olgu sügisel
tagasi siin kirevate kivide lahes
Udus säragu nende sarved
ja sädelegu teie silmad
Aga südamed hoidke selged ja jahedad
nagu hommikukaste

Teie ei harju iial inimnaiste eluga
see paneb südamele kütked
unistused ei täitu
ja tunnetest tõuseb vaid tuska
Inimesed on ilusad aga julmad
Nad hoiavad peredesse nagu putukad
korjavad öösiti unede kulda
ja hommikul pillavad kõik käest

Saada neist kellegi omaks tähendab olla
ühele inimtähele ähvardavalt lähedal

Aga teie silmad on nagu ilmameri
tähed upuvad sinna

¶

Cows come from the sea
on this morning at the beginning of time
blue-green cows
udders full of salty sea milk
and the Sea Mother drives them ashore
with a switch of sea-grass

Sea Maidens come keep the cows
and keep yourselves
from lecherous herders by night
In autumn may a hundred blue-green cows
be back here in the bay between mottled stones
May their horns glisten in the mist
and may your eyes sparkle
But keep your hearts clear and cool
like the morning dew

You will never get used to the life of human women
it puts fetters on the heart
dreams are never fulfilled
and feelings only give rise to grief
People are beautiful but cruel
They keep to their kin like insects
they gather the gold of dreams by night
squander it all away in the morning

To become someone's own means being
dangerously close to a human star

But your eyes are like the sea of the world
stars drown in it

Merineitsid tulge lehmi hoidma
Aga südamed hoidke selged ja jahedad
nagu hommikukaste

Sea Maidens come keep the cows
But keep your hearts clear and cool
like the morning dew

¶

Kaldapääsukesed merekivimustad
röövkajakad rannavahuvalged
kiljute sadama kohal
sööstate üle kirikute
tiirlete kohal linnamüüri
murdlainete ja minu
linnud linnalinnud
mida te pajatate Tallinnast

Räägite ju
kuidas siin hädakelli löödi
kuidas emad lastega jooksid
kui kõikjal olid müürid ees
ja Vene pommilennukid tulid ja tulid
ida poolt peale
kui kõik põles karjus ja varises
pragunes ja lõhkes

Kuulen praegu veel nuttu
selle kivise keskaegse kaunitari
iidvana linna
leinakleitide kahinat
tunnen tuult
vaigistavat pehmet olevikutuult
mis lennutab sulgi ja liiva

¶

Sand martins sea-stone black
gulls sea-foam white
you screech over the harbour
sweep over the churches
circle over the city walls
the breaking waves and me
birds city birds
what tales do you tell of Tallinn

You tell of
how the the alarm bells were rung
how mothers ran with their children
when everywhere walls were in the way
and the Russian bombers kept coming and coming
from the east
when it was all burning screaming and crumbling
cracking and bursting

Even now I hear the weeping
this stony medieval beauty's
this age-old city's
black dresses rustling
I feel the wind
the soothing soft wind of the present
that makes feathers and sand fly

¶

Laps mängib
punaste Hiina laternatega
oma vanavanaisa toas

Vanavanaisa on siit ammu läinud
Nüüd on see tuba panipaik
aga ma tahaksin nii väga
anda sellele toale uut elu

No näiteks see kolakas riidekapp
täis vanu kasukaid ja tekke
ja kapi ning laua vahele kiilutud õmblusmasin
mis ei lase kapiust lahti teha

Ja see nõuka-aegne lakitud kirjutuslaud
mis ei lase õmblusmasinat akna poole nihutada
Jah see kirjutuslaud
täis vanu kviitungeid
ema turkmeeni keele konspekte
ja vanavanaema laulukladesid
halearmsas ilukirjas laulusõnu
    Minu venna mõrtsukas
    ja *Liisa – petis pruut*
tolmuimejate ja muruniidukite passe
kärtslillasid kopeerpabereid
millega me õega laulva revolutsiooni päevil
oma heledad poisipead punksiniseks nühkisime
vanu lõikelehti ürgaegsete moodidega
Kirjutuslaud täis helearmast paberiprahti
laud kus taga keegi kunagi ei istu
Ja siis veel see tuttavatelt saadud kappriiul

¶

The child plays
with red Chinese lanterns
in his great-grandfather's room

Great-grandfather is long since gone
Now this room is a box-room
but I would so very much like
to give this room new life

For example this massive clothes cupboard
full of old coats and blankets
and wedged in between cupboard and table the sewing machine
that doesn't allow the cupboard door to open

And this Soviet-time lacquered writing table
that won't allow the sewing machine to be shifed towards the window
Yes this writing table
full of old receipts
Mother's Turkmen language notes
and Great-grandmother's notebooks full of songs
song lyrics in her poignantly sweet handwriting
        My brother's murderer
        and *Liisa – deceitful bride*
vacuum cleaner and lawnmower manuals
screaming violet carbon paper
with which my sister and I rubbed our fair boyish heads
punk-blue in the days of the singing revolution
old sewing patterns of ancient fashions
The writing table full of such dear scraps of paper
the table nobody ever sits at
And then there's that cupboard from acquaintances

täis plaate mida keegi kunagi ei kuula
Ja need üksteise peale laotud pappkastid nurgas
täis Nõukogude Naisi Pikreid ja Eesti Loodust
Kuhu siin inimesed peaksid mahtuma

Oleksin ma siin majas ometi võõras
viskaksin vilistades minema vanad kasukad
ja selle kirjutuslaua
nihutaksin *Singeri* akna alla
kingiksin ära plaadid mida keegi kunagi ei kuula
paneksin ajakirjad pööningule ära
tooksin sisse oma suured lilled
vaibad ja põrandalambi
mõned raamatud
Ja kõik

Aga ei
Sääraseid asju võõrad ei või
aga liiga lähedased ei saa teha
Nad on otsekui halvatud
mälestuste ja asjaolude külge aheldatud

Oleksin ma ometi võõras
teeksin siin kõik mängeldes korda
puhuksin siia uue eluvaimu sisse
Aga mu süda ütleb
et tuleb olla õrn ja ettevaatlik siin
mälestuste toas
tuleb arvestada asjaoludega
Mälestused on haprad nagu Hiina laternad
Ometi on need täna
tugevamad kui mu tahe

full of records that nobody ever listens to
And those cardboard boxes in the corner
stacked one upon the other full of old Soviet magazines
How are people supposed to fit in here

If I were a stranger in this house
I'd be whistling while I threw the old coats out
and this writing table
I'd shift the Singer under the window
give away the records nobody ever listens to
put the magazines in the loft
I'd bring in my big plants
carpets and floor lamp
some books
And that's it

But no
Strangers aren't allowed to do such things
but those who are too close aren't able to
It's as if they're paralyzed
shackled to memories and circumstances

Yet if I were a stranger
It would be child's play to put everything here in order
I'd breathe a new spirit of life in
But my heart tells me
to be gentle and careful here
in this room of memories
to consider the circumstances
Memories are as fragile as Chinese lanterns
Yet today they are
stronger than my will

II
YOUR EYES INSIDE ME

SU SILMAD MU SEES

¶

Ootan sind seiklejat rännuhullu
keeran krepppaberist kollaseid roose
ümber vasktraadi
kütan kaminat
selle armutult külma
veebruaripäeva auks
Tunnen su liigutusi
tasast tugevat tulemist
minu poole
minu maailma poole
läbi tuisu

Oled ammu juba olemas
ometi olemata
Oleme vaadanud teineteise silmadesse
vaid unes
Su silmad mu sees
suu mu sees
Südagi siinsamas
lähemal kui miski muu

¶

I wait for you adventurer mad rover
I wind yellow crêpe paper roses
round copper wire
put wood on the fire
in honour of this pitilessly cold
February day
I feel your movements
your slow strong coming
towards me
towards my world
through the snowstorm

You're already there long since
and yet you aren't
We've looked into each other's eyes
only in dreams
your eyes inside me
your mouth inside me
your heart right here
closer than anything else

¶

Sellel ööl
kui alevimajade aiateibad praksusid
30-kraadise pakase käes
ja jääpurikad
rippusid pikkade piikidena
haigla katuseräästast alla
Sel küünlakuuööl
ärkasin kuuetunnise lapsukese kõrval
kuulatasin
kas ta ikka hingab
Näha ei olnud midagi
Katsusin
siis tekkide sees
ta pisikest sooja ninaotsa
ja tundsin
kuidas selle planeedi ääretul
emaarmastuse põllul
puhkes õide
ka minu südame
tumepunane moon

Ja südaöiti
kui ärkan taas
et lapse ninaotsa katsuda
tunnen selle vereva lille
magusat murelikku lõhna

¶

In that night
when the fence-posts of the market-town houses
cracked in the minus 30 degree cold
and icicles
hung down like long lances
from the eaves of the hospital
In that February night
I woke up beside my six hour-old child
listened
if he was still breathing
There was nothing to be seen
I touched
the tiny warm tip of his nose
inside the blankets
and felt
how on this planet's boundless
field of a mother's love
the dark red poppy
of my heart
burst into blossom

And in the heart of night
when I wake again
to touch
the tip of my child's nose
I feel the sweet anxious scent
of that blood-red flower

¶

Enam ei anna ma sulle rinda
Õunapuud on teist korda su elus õisi täis
Uinutan sind magama meie aia
esimese ja ainsa antoonovka all
ja su lutipudelis loksub mahl
sellestsamast puust

mahl üle-eelmisest sügisest
kui olime alles üks
kui ma polnud veel päriselt ema
ja sina veel päriselt laps

Tahan olla siin
sinu suur ja sitke
antoonovkalõhnaline ema
Päriselt ema
kuigi enam ei anna ma sulle rinda
sulle
päriselt minu laps

¶

I don't give you my breast anymore
The apple trees are in blossom for the second time in your life
I lull you to sleep beneath our garden's
first and only Antonovka apple tree
and the juice sloshing around in your baby-bottle
is from that very same tree

Juice from the autumn before last
when we were still one
when I wasn't really a mother yet
and you weren't really a child

Here I want to be
your big sinewy
mother smelling of Antonovka
Really your mother
even though I don't give you my breast anymore
you
really my child

¶

Laps turnib aknalaual
Ühe käega hoian teda kukkumast
teisega kirjutan
Hommik on käima läinud
tee joodud puder söödud
sirelid ära õitsenud
pojengide viimased pungad
löövad valla

Öösel lõhnasid need mu tuppa
Laps magas
suu leivapurune
Teadsin korraga et see
saja haarmega mu külge keerdunud
kohustustepundar
ongi mu elu

Ometi olin õnnelik
kui laps magas
ja pojengid lõhnasid läbi sääsevõrgu
mu tuppa

¶

My child clambers on the windowsill
With one hand I keep him from falling
with the other I write
Morning has started up
tea drunk porridge eaten
lilacs gone to seed
the peonies' last buds
open up

In the night their scent came into my room
My child slept
his mouth covered with bread crumbs
All at once I knew that this
bundle of responsibilities
entwined to me by a hundred arms
is my life

And I was happy
as my child slept
and the scent of peonies drifted through the mosquito net
into my room

¶

Tunda on valgete hobuste lõhna
Marmortreppidel vihmavesi
libe ja ohtlik
Viigimarjad
küpsed nagu minu
viha sinu vastu

Külm päikeseloojangu hetk
kus keegi ei kuku kellegi
käte vahele
Isegi ema ja laps
vaatavad üksi
oma unede sügavasse
orgu

Ema kes on alati
täiskohaga ema
Laps kes on veel
põhjatult laps

Ärkame
Priske lilla päevatriip
öötaevas
meelitab meid välja
Kärutan lapsega
Jumalaema orgu

Tähti kukub
kruusateele tükkideks
Laternavalgus paneb möödujate seelikud
lehvima
Meeste silmad tunduvad eriti mustad

¶

The smell of white horses can be felt
Rainwater on the marble steps
slippery and dangerous
Figs
as ripe as my
anger against you

The cold moment of sunset
where nobody falls into
anyone's arms
Even mother and child
look alone
into the deep valley of their
dreams

A mother who is always
a full-time mother
A child who is still
utterly a child

We wake
A glowing purple streak of day
in the night sky
entices us out
I wheel the child
into the valley of the mother of God

Stars fall
into pieces on the gravel road
Lantern light makes the skirts of passers-by
flutter
Mens' eyes appear especially black

Olen tühi
lilla taevatriibu ilust
jumalaema hobustest
ja sinu varju lõhnast
oru põhjas

I am empty
from the beauty of the purple streak in the sky
the horses of the mother of God
and the scent of your shadow
at the bottom of the valley

¶

Mu puhkus oli lühike
Jõudsin vaevalt kohale
kui hakkasin tagasi sõitma
Laps oli kodus haigeks jäänud

Sõitsin tagasi
Vahepeal tukkusin
Ärkasin
Kuulatasin
oma rahutult tuksuvat emasüdant
Olin nagu hunt ennast valuga kupeesse
kerra tõmmanud
Rongikardina tagant
nägin suurt suvekuud
Vilksamisi märkasin
Kesk-Soome samblasi metsaaluseid
Kaugemal kupees nuttis laps
aga varsti ta juba laulis
Lugesin peatusi
minuteid
oma südametukseid

Hommikul Helsingis kiirustasin sadamasse
kaks umbkeelset Jaapani turisti kannul
Nemadki tahtsid Tallinna
Aitasin nad õigesse terminaali
õigesse kassasse
õigele laevale
Nemad aitasid mul hetkeks unustada

On Vana Tallinna
suur allahindlus

¶

My holiday was short
I had barely arrived
when I started travelling back
My child had fallen ill at home

I travelled back
In between I dozed
Woke up
Listened
to my restlessly beating mother's heart
I was like a wolf curled up
in pain in the compartment
From behind the curtain
I saw the big summer moon
I caught glimpses of
Central Finland's mossy forest floor
Further along in a compartment a child cried
but before long was singing
I counted the stops
the minutes
the beats of my heart

In the morning in Helsinki I rushed to the harbour
at my heels two Japanese tourists without the language
They wanted to go to Tallinn too
I helped them to the right terminal
the right ticket window
the right ferry
They helped me to forget for a moment

There's a big sale
on Vana Tallinn liqueur

ja Viru Valge uudistoodete
kampaania
Lasen seljatoe alla
lasen merel end õõtsutada
Astun esimesena laevast maha
kannul viina- ja naisteküttide
hordid
ning kaks vaatamisväärsustenäljas
Jaapani turisti

Istun rooli
sõidan ikka veel varavalges
Viru väravatest mööda
Jätan seljataha vana Tallinna tuttavad teed
Harjumaa tuttavad metsad
Enne Hagudit on alkokontroll
Peatun
Puhun
Saan loa edasi sõita

Olin ometi võtnud
sel pikal koduteel
võtnud rüübet
kõigi maailma emade armastuse ja kannatuse
karikast

Kogu kampaania viinad
on selle kõrval lahja lake
Kõik allahindluse joogid
jäävad alla
sellele sõõmule

and a campaign for new Viru Valge vodka products
I let the back of my seat down
and let the sea rock me
I'm the first one off the ferry
hordes hunting drink and women
at my heels
and two Japanese tourists
hungering for the sights

I sit behind the wheel
drive in the still-early brightness
past Viru Gate
leave behind me the familiar streets of old Tallinn
the familar forests of Harjumaa
Before Hagudi the police are checking for drink-drivers
I stop
I blow
I get permission to drive on

And yet I'd had a drink
on that long road home
I'd had a drink
from the goblet
of the love and perseverence of all the world's mothers

All the sales campaign vodka
is a watery swill beside that
All the marked down drink
won't measure up to a draught
of that

¶

Lumi mäletab mu turja
puusi pahkluid
Kandsin teda kaua endaga kaasas
siis ei osanud ma veel
kirjutadagi

Tol ajal olid tähed viisakamad
ja soojemad
Nad teretasid mind
kui läksin üksi
alasti oma lumega

Tähed polnud siis veel hiigelpäikesed
kaugel avakosmoses
Nad olid tillukesed sõbralikud
valgusetäpid
mis ilmusid õhtuti äkitselt
talvetaeva põhjatusse nõkku
vaatasid sisse mu imetlusest pärani
silmapõhjadesse
peegeldades mu lund
mu avali alastiolekut
mis oligi kaitse

¶

The snow remembers my shoulders
my hips my ankles
I carried it with me a long time
I didn't even know how
to write yet then

The stars were more courteous then
and warmer
They greeted me
when I went alone
naked with my snow

The stars weren't giant suns yet then
in the distant expanse of the cosmos
They were tiny friendly
spots of light
that suddenly appeared in the evening
in the bottomless hollow of the winter sky
and looked into the bottom of my eyes
wide open in admiration
reflecting my snow
my open nakedness
that was my shield

III
RAVEN AND SUN
RONKA JA PÄIKEST

¶

Kihutan sinu poole
üle Aafrika
all Kameruni sadamate tuled ja
Burkina Faso pilkane pimedus

Ilusad ploomikarva naised tulevad turult
kirjud kannud pealael
lapsed sagimas ümber säärte

Kihutan sinu poole
läbi Sahara
Sahisen nagu uss läbi liiva
Kihutan üle hiigel-Niiluse
mis jälgib mind näljaselt
hõõrudes oma märgi külgi
vastu januseid kaldaid

Sööstan su poole
üle Kuldsarve lahe
läbi ajaloo
läbi tuhande ja ühe sügise ja talve
läbi ööde
mida peaaegu polnudki olemas
läbi oliivisalude
läbi magusalt lõhnavate
viinamarjapõldude
kannad kahisemas vastu kevadet
patsid lohisemas vastu suurt suve

Kihutan sinu poole üle
palavate paavstimaade

¶

I career along towards you
across Africa
down below Cameroon's harbour lights and
Burkina Faso's impenetrable darkness

Beautiful plum-coloured women come from the market
mottled jugs on their heads
children scurrying round their shins

I career along towards you
through the Sahara
swish like a snake through the sand
I career over the giant Nile
that tracks me hungrily
rubbing its wet sides
against the thirsty banks

I sweep towards you
over Golden Horn Bay
through history
through a thousand and one autumns and winters
through nights
that nearly never were
through olive groves
through sweet-smelling
fields of grapes
heels swishing towards spring
plaits trailing behind towards high summer

I career along towards you over
hot papal lands

kus patud päevitavad
iga armastuse kraavis
Kas kuuled kuidas ma tulen
mina musta Eeva
äkitselt valge võsu

Mu rinnad kumavad nagu klaariõunad
randmed on rahutud nagu
hilissuverohi

Kihutan su poole
üle Baltimaade
tanklate ja traataedade
külade ja kruusateede
üle kokku laenatud kodude
ja liisinguautode mere

Kihutan su külla
täielikku tagalasse
ja mu juuksed ja sall õhkuvad ikka veel
hilissuvehurma

Kihutan läbi
aastasadade
sumpan põlvkondade mülgastes
tulen neutraalselt ja elusalt
kõigist sõdadest läbi

Tulen värisemata üle
üksilduselahtede
et haista su lõhna
mõõta kallistustega su õlgade laiust

where sins sun themselves
in the ditch of every love
Do you hear me coming
me Black African Eve's
suddenly white offshoot

My breasts are aglow like yellow apples
my wrists are restless like
late summer grass

I career towards you
over the Baltic lands
petrol stations and wire fences
villages and gravel roads
over houses borrowed for
and a sea of leased cars

I career over to your village
far from the front
and my hair and scarf still emanate
the spell of late summer

I career through
centuries
wade through the quagmire of generations
come neutral and alive
through all wars

I come without trembling over
bays of loneliness
to smell you
to measure with embraces the breadth of your shoulders

Sina
noor vana
kerge raske
igivana rahuliku rahva
mässav poeg

Mina
musta Eeva
äkitselt valge võsu
rinnad nagu Peipsi sibulad
silmad ujedad nagu
Läänemere särjed
pilk kindel nagu
ei miski siin ilmas

Juba oled sa lähedal
Su sõrmede ümber on pimedus
su südame ümber sõda
Oled ilus ja soolane
ja sääsed sind ei söö

You
young old
light heavy
rebellious son
of an age-old peaceful people

I
Black African Eve's
suddenly white offshoot
breasts like Peipus onions
eyes shy like
Baltic Sea roach
a sure gaze like
nothing else in this world

Already you are close
darkness around your fingers
war around your heart
you are beautiful and salty
and the mosquitos do not bite you

¶

Võtan pruudikleidi seljast
esimest ja viimast korda

Öö sõrmil seljal
Vihm visklemas
vastu rõduäärt
Pargis huikamas tiirased paabulinnukuked

                    kuaaak-kuaaak

Saan trukid valla
libistan luku lahti
Juba langeb siid
üle mu piha kõhu ja jalge
kukub kahinal põrandale maha
Jälle huikavad linnud
jälle kisavad kuked

                    kuaaak-kuaaak

Avan õhuakna tuleakna ja veeakna
katuseakna ja keldriakna
välisukse ja siseukse
ja libisen uude kirevasulelisse rüüsse
löön saba valla
ja kogun endasse kogu selle öö kire
leina ja vihma

Ei saa minust punast
ühemõõtmelist pruuti
selles paganlikus öös

¶

I take off my bridal dress
for the first and last time

Night in my fingers on my back
Rain thrashing
against the balcony
In the park lustful peacocks calling

        quaaack-quaaack

I get the snaps undone
and slide the zip down
And already the silk slips down
over my waist stomach and legs
falls rustling onto the floor
again the birds call
again the cocks cry

        quaaack-quaaack

I open the airing window fire window and water window
roof window and cellar window
outside door and inside door
and slip into new many-coloured feathered raiment
unfurl my tail
and gather into myself all of this night's passion
sorrow and rain

I will never become a blushing
one-dimensional bride
on this pagan night

Jään vaatamata valgele kleidile
kombele ja seadusele
suleliste inimlaste ilmalekandjaks

I remain regardless of the white dress
custom and law
the bearer of feathered hominids into the world

¶

Su saarepuud
olid samblakollased
su õuemuru just roheliseks läinud
ja meie olime just õide läinud
Linnud olid purjus
ja oja tahtis
tahtis üle kallaste
ja kuu oli nii täis
et pidi peaaegu lõhkema
Panin pea
su peopessa
kuulasin sookurgede armulaulu
taga su ürgmetsade

Vanad kaevu- ja korstnakohad
jäid tähistama elu
Üks ikka veel kustumata
päikesetäht
jäi hõõguma
meie maailma kohale

¶

Your ash trees
were moss-yellow
the grass in your yard just gone green
and we had just burst into blossom
The birds were drunk
and the stream wanted
wanted to overflow its banks
and the moon was so full
that it nearly had to burst
I nested my head
in the palm of your hand
and listened to the cranes' love song
beyond your primeval forests

Old sites of wells and chimneys
stayed to mark life
One still unextinguished
solar star
stayed to glow
over our world

¶

Las trammid kaovad
taamal teetolmu
las kajakad liuglevad
Stockmanni Hullude Päevade kohal
nagu lastelennukid
Las pajud ajavad urbi
ja lumi jätab endast viimaseid
haledaid laike

Komeedikommipaki ja kasemahlapudeliga
istume noorte mändide alla maha
keset käbisid ja liiva
paiselehti ja kive
parki linnamüüri taha

Mul on hariliku pliiatsi karva silmad
ja käeseljad suudlusi täis
Sul on punane lõng ümber käe
ja käed ümber minu
Ma õitsen ja valutan
pikkade paekivikarva juuste all
ja meie südamed on selle maavaratu Maarjamaa
viimased põlevkivitükid

Varsti lõpevad needki
Me ärkame surmaunest
suurte suguvõsade viisi
ajame varred sirgu
harutame keeled sõlmest lahti

¶

Let the trams disappear
in the distant dust
let the seagulls soar
over Stockmann's Store Mad Days sale
like childrens' planes
Let the willows grow catkins
and the snow leave a few last pitiful patches
of itself

With a packet of Komeet sweets and a bottle of birch juice
we sit down under the young pines
amid pine cones and sand
coltsfoot and stones
in the park behind the city wall.

I have eyes the colour of a common pencil
and the backs of my hands full of kisses
You have red yarn round your hand
and your hands round me
I blossom and ache
under long hair the colour of limestone
and in this mineral-poor Land of Mary
this Estonia
our hearts are the last pieces
of burning shale

Soon even they will be gone
We wake from a deathly sleep
in the way of great tribes one after another
stretch our limbs out straight
untangle our tongues from their knots

Globaalküla kutsub meid kokku
ühe elektrikamina ette
Ja kujutlus tulest
seob meie sooned ja südamed

The global village calls us together
in front of an electric fireplace
And the notion of fire
binds our veins and our hearts

¶

Terve kuhi kulda
on pudenenud
vahtra alla selle tänava lõpus
Vaher ise jäi raagu
jäi tühjaks ja lagedaks nagu taevas
Kõik pilved on hirmunult pagenud tuule eest
mis sööstab üle lageda

Vaikus
Mõni mädand paradiisiõun kukub
vastu Fordi esiklaasi
Mõni minevikuvari
mõni unistus meenutab
et kõik võiks olla veel täiuslikum

Üldiselt on rõske ja hirmus
leegitsevate mürgimarjade ja
roostes veerennide
sügis
Armastan raudrohtu
mis õitseb külmasüdameni välja
Vihkan ainult varrukaid
ja kindaid
Liiga tüütu on toppida neisse
oma sitkeid oksaharulisi
käsi

On viimaste veerandtundide õhtu
Ammu juba olen süüdanud oma südame
punased pidurituled
aga need neetud näivad
sind eriti ligi meelitavat

¶

A whole pile of gold
has settled
under the maple at the end of this street
The maple itself has been left bare
left empty and open as the sky
All the clouds have fled in fear from the wind
sweeping over the open fields

Silence
Some rotting paradise apple falls
against the Ford's windscreen
Some shadow of the past
some reverie reminds me
that everything could be even more whole

By and large it's a damp and dreadful
autumn
of blazing poison berries
and rusted gutters
I love yarrow
that blossoms into the heart of the cold
I only despise sleeves
and gloves
So troublesome to stuff
my tough branchy hands
into them

It is the evening of final quarter hours
Long ago I'd already lit my heart's
red brake-lights
but the blasted things seem
to entice you especially close

Stopp
Kuluvärvi kõrred
rabapalavik
kolm rebase- ja kolm kährikulaipa maanteel
Laukajärv kuhu on hea
otse saunast
aga võib ka niisama
novembrilõhn kopsudes
kõhuli laudtee tipus
pista käed küünarnukist saati
näha hetkeks oma nägu
külmumiseelses maailmas

Jää suleb järvede laud
Laudtee lõpus
põlen igatsusest tõelise enda järele
Või on see vaid virvatuli
lubamas meelitamas
kutsumas mind veel enne ööd
enne jääkaane kukkumist
suure soo peale
madalale marduste ja mardikate
maale

Stop
Stubble the colour of dead grass
marsh fever
the corpses of three foxes
and three raccoon dogs on the road
A bog lake it's so good to get into
straight from the sauna
but with the scent of November in your lungs
on your stomach at the tip of the wooden path
you can just as well
stick your hands in up to the elbow
see your face for a moment
in a world soon to be frozen over

Ice closes the lakes' eyelids
At the end of the wooden path
I burn with yearning for the real me
or is that just a will o' the wisp
promising enticing
calling me before night
before the cover of ice falls
onto the great marsh
to the low land
of wraiths and chafers

ÄRALEND

Oma õrna koort
sinu vastu lauldes
oma hiigelviiuli jõhve
sinu vastu saagides
tõusin su juurest üles taevasse
su juurte juurest
kõrgete kuuselatvade kohale
su kõrvade kõrvalt
sinisesse laotusse

Vaatasin alla
su unise katuse peale
kadusin
kõrvad lukus
uni kurgus kinni
taha pilvede

Ometi sinu juures
sinu juurte juures
oli taevas taevam

FLYING AWAY

Singing my delicate
shell against you
sawing my giant fiddle's
bow against you
I rose from where you were into the sky
from where you were rooted
up over the fir tree tops
from beside you at your ear
up into the blue expanse

I looked down
at your sleepy roof
With my ears locked
sleep stuck in my throat
I disappeared
behind the clouds

Yet where you were
where you were rooted
the sky was more sky-like

¶

Meil kõigil tuleb harjuda
aeglase surmaga
Meist kõigist saavad vähehaaval kondikujud
kuuvalgel aasal
tuhk ohvrikivi lohus

Kui sinu peale vihastan
siis mõtlen ikka
sinu luukere peale
ja see lepitab

On kooljakuu ilusaim päev
ja päike limpsab hetkeks meie
kahvatuid palgeid

Sa valad natuke mürki klaasidesse
natuke varju valgusesse
Igal öösel näitan sulle millimeetri võrra rohkem
oma valget säär

On heinakuu haljaim aeg
Igal hommikul heidan end natuke kauemaks
Surnumere soola
rüüpan natuke julgemalt su tunnete tulikaleotist
su suudluste ussilakaleent

Meil kõigil tuleb harjuda

¶

We all have to grow accustomed
to a slow death
we will all gradually become figures of bone
in a moonlit meadow
dust in the hollow of a sacrificial stone

When I get angry with you
I always think
about your skeleton
and that reconciles

It is the loveliest day of November
the month of the dead
and for a moment the sun licks
our pale faces

You pour a bit of poison into the glasses
a bit of shadow into the light
Every night I show you a millimetre more
of my white leg

It is the greenest time of July
the month of haymaking
Every morning I lay myself down a bit longer
in the salt of the Dead Sea
sip the steeped buttercups of your feelings a bit more boldly
the herb Paris brew of your kisses

We all have to grow accustomed

¶

Aed on täis
mu valgete jalgade laulu

Hing on nagu need ämblikuniidid
risti-rästi
pingul
kahe klaariõunapuu vahel

Enne koitu
on kehad rasked
uni surub laud sügavale alla
Sa magad
ripsmed puhkamas põskedel
hommik pole veel puudutanud su unede põlde
su alateadvuse üksildasi lauskmaid

Maga-maga
käed ümber minu
Siin on ohutu öö
Aed on risti-rästi täis
ämblikuniite
ja mu valgete jalgade laulu

¶

The garden is full
of the song of my white feet

My soul is like these threads of spider silk
tensed
criss-cross
between two apple trees

Before dawn
bodies are heavy
sleep presses eyelids down
You sleep
eyelashes resting on your cheeks
morning has not yet touched the fields of your dreams
the lonely open land of your subconscious

Sleep-sleep
your arms around me
Here the night is safe and sound
The garden is criss-cross full
of spider silk
and the song of my white feet

¶

Vaatad mulle otsa
nagu perule hobusele
Tee ääres kollased ogalilled
kollased võililled
ja raps
Minagi olen kollase ja musta segu

Sinus on musta ja valget ja ussilakasinist
aga ei kübetki kollast

Vaatad mulle otsa nagu perule hobusele
tõstad mu lõuga oma käega
sasid lakka
ja turja

Minus on kollast ja musta
ja ronka ja päikest

Kraaksatan ja kappan minema
sest ma ei tea
kas sa tead et see
kes taltsutab
vastutab

Võiksin sind ju ka
turjale võtta
et tunneksid mu sitkust
mu ronka ja päikest
musta ja kollast
mu sametist märga märakarva
mu tugevat emandaturja

¶

You look at me
as you would a skittish horse
At the side of the road yellow thorny flowers
yellow dandelions
and rape blossoms
Even I am a mix of yellow and black

In you there is black and white and herb-Paris-blue
but not even a speck of yellow

You look at me as you would a skittish horse
you lift my chin with your hand
you tousle my mane
and withers

In me there is yellow and black
and raven and sun

I caw and gallop away
for I don't know
if you know that he
who tames
answers for it

I could take you
on my withers
and make you feel my fibre
my raven and sunlight
black and yellow
my wet velvet mare's fur
my strong woman's shoulders

aga ma ei tea
kas ma tean
et see kes kannab
ka vastutab

Sellepärast pagen
õhku ahmides
õhtuhämaras
läbi maailma suurima laane
Istun maailma
ilusaima vaatega künkale
vanade puude alla maha
ise ikka nii pigimust
nii tulikakollane

Kas tundsid
kuidas ma sind vaatasin
Su silmad olid kinni kinni kinni
Kas mäletad magnooliaid
mõni õis oli nii suur
et oleksime sinna peaaegu ära mahtunud
Õhk oli soolane
magus ja valus

Mõõtsid mõõgaga mere sügavust
käega mu juuste pehmust
huultega unistusi
Suvi läbi olin sind oodanud
paljajalu
hallil soojal
lävepakukivil

but I don't know
if I know
that she who carries
answers for it

That's why I flee
huffing for air
in the evening dusk
through the world's greatest forest
I sit down
under the old trees on the hill
with the world's most beautiful view
myself still so pitch black
so buttercup yellow

Did you feel
how I watched you
Your eyes were closed closed closed
Do you remember the magnolias
some blossoms were so big
that we would almost have fit
The air was salty
sweet and painful

You measured the depth of the sea with a sword
the softness of my hair with your hand
dreams with your lips
All summer long I had waited for you
barefoot
on a warm grey
stone on the threshhold

Suvi läbi oodanud sind
koju

Hea nii hea oleks jälle naerda
Sest ma ei usu enam
et kes naerab
see nutab
Hea nii hea oleks jälle nutta
sest ma usun veel
et kes nutab
see armastab

Öö aus öö
kihutavate mootorrataste
ja rumalate rooside öö

Me kihutame mööda
ja mul on kinni hoida millestki
mägisügavast
millestki orgkõrgest

Öö aus öö

See on meie märg mõnus
võrgust välja libisev
soe
elu
jäämäe jalamil

All summer long I had waited for you
to come home

It would be good so good to laugh again
For I no longer believe
that whoever laughs
cries
It would be so good to cry again
for I still believe
that whoever cries
loves

Night honest night
night of speeding motorbikes
and frivolous roses

We speed along
and I have something to hold on to
that is mountain-deep
valley-high

Night honest night

This is our wet pleasant
warm
life
slipping out of the net
at the foot of the iceberg

Kristiina Ehin was born in Rapla, Estonia in 1977. She received an M. A. in Comparative and Estonian Folklore from Tartu University in 2004. She has published five volumes of poetry in her native Estonia and has won a number of prizes there, including Estonia's most prestigious poetry prize for her fourth volume, written during a year spent as a nature reserve warden on an uninhabited island off Estonia's north coast. She has also published a book of short stories and has written a play as well. *The Drums of Silence* (Oleander Press, Cambridge, 2007), a volume of her selected poems in English translation, was awarded the Poetry Society Corneliu M. Popescu Prize for European Poetry in Translation in 2007. Her other books in English translation are *Põletades pimedust – Burning the Darkness – An Dorchadas á Dhó* (trilingual Estonian-English-Irish selected poems, Coiscéim, Dublin, 2009), *A Priceless Nest*, (short stories, Oleander Press, Cambridge, 2009), *Päevaseiskaja – South-Estonian Fairy Tales* (Huma, Tallinn, 2009) and *Noorkuuhommik – New Moon Morning* (selected poems, Huma, Tallinn, 2007). She is often invited to take part in international arts and literary festivals and her work, poetry and prose, appears regularly in English translation in leading Irish and British literary journals. Her work has been translated into twelve languages.

The poems in *The Scent of Your Shadow* have been selected from her most recent book, entitled *Emapuhkus*, published in April 2009. The poems were written over a period of two years beginning shortly before the birth of her child.

Ilmar Lehtpere had a bilingual upbringing in Estonian and English. He is the translator of Kristiina Ehin's *The Drums of Silence* (Oleander Press, Cambridge, 2007), which was awarded the Poetry Society Corneliu M. Popescu Prize for European Poetry in Translation. His other translations of Kristiina Ehin's work are *Põletades pimedust – Burning the Darkness – An Dorchadas á Dhó* (trilingual Estonian-English-Irish selected poems, Coiscéim, Dublin, 2009), *A Priceless Nest*, (short stories, Oleander Press, Cambridge, 2009), *Päevaseiskaja – South-Estonian Fairy Tales* (Huma, Tallinn, 2009) and *Noorkuuhommik – New Moon Morning* (selected poems, Huma, Tallinn, 2007). He has also translated her play, *A Life Without Feathers*, and has already started working on her next collection of poems in English. His translations of Kristiina Ehin's poetry and prose appear regularly in leading Irish and British literary journals. His own poetry has appeared in Estonian and Irish literary journals.

SUJATA BHATT was born in Ahmedabad, India, and grew up in Pune, India and in the United States. To date, she has published seven collections of poetry with Carcanet Press. The recipient of numerous awards, such as the Commonwealth Poetry Prize (Asia), and the Cholmondeley Award, her latest collection, *Pure Lizard*, was short-listed for the Forward Poetry Prize and received the German Literature Award, *Das neue Buch*, in 2008. She has translated poetry from Gujarati and German into English. Her work has been widely anthologised, broadcast on radio and television, and has been translated into more than twenty languages. She is a frequent guest at literary festivals throughout the world. Currently, she lives in Germany with her family.

No. 11 – YANNIS KONDOS (Greece)
Absurd Athlete
Translated by David Connolly, introduced by David Constantine

No. 12 – BEJAN MATUR (Turkey)
In the Temple of a Patient God
Translated by Ruth Christie, introduced by Maureen Freely

No. 13 – GABRIEL FERRATER (Catalonia / Spain)
Women and Days
Translated by Arthur Terry, introduced by Seamus Heaney

No. 14 – INNA LISNIANSKAYA (Russia)
Far from Sodom
Translated by Daniel Weissbort, introduced by Elaine Feinstein

No. 15 – SABINE LANGE (Germany)
The Fishermen Sleep
Translated by Jenny Williams, introduced by Mary O'Donnell

No. 16 – TAKAHASHI MUTSUO (Japan)
We of Zipangu
Translated by James Kirkup & Tamaki Makoto, introduced by Glyn Pursglove

No. 17 – JURIS KRONBERGS (Latvia)
Wolf One-Eye
Translated by Mara Rozitis, introduced by Jaan Kaplinski

No. 18 – REMCO CAMPERT (Holland)
I Dreamed in the Cities at Night
Translated by Donald Gardner, introduced by Paul Vincent

No. 19 – DOROTHEA ROSA HERLIANY (Indonesia)
Kill the Radio
Translated by Harry Aveling, introduced by Linda France

No. 20 – SOLEÏMAN ADEL GUÉMAR (Algeria)
State of Emergency
Translated by Tom Cheesman & John Goodby, introduced by Lisa Appignanesi
(PEN Translation Award)

No. 21 – ELI TOLARETXIPI (Spain / Basque)
Still Life with Loops
Translated by Philip Jenkins, introduced by Robert Crawford

No. 22 – FERNANDO KOFMAN (Argentina)
The Flights of Zarza
Translated by Ian Taylor, introduced by Andrew Graham Yooll

No. 23 – LARISSA MILLER (Russia)
Guests of Eternity
Translated by Richard McKane, introduced by Sasha Dugdale
(Poetry Book Society Recommended Translation)

No. 24 – ANISE KOLTZ (Luxembourg)
At the Edge of Night
Translated by Anne-Marie Glasheen, introduced by Caroline Price

No. 25 – MAURICE CARÊME (Belgium)
Defying Fate
Translated by Christopher Pilling, introduced by Martin Sorrell

No. 26 – VALÉRIE ROUZEAU (France)
Cold Spring in Winter
Translated by Susan Wicks, introduced by Stephen Romer

No. 27 – RAZMIK DAVOYAN (France)
Whispers and Breath of the Meadows
Translated by Arminé Tamrazian, introduced by W. N. Herbert

No. 28 – FRANÇOIS JACQMIN (Belgium)
The Book of the Snow
Translated by Philip Mosely, introduced by Clive Scott